CW00741347

It's Easy To Play Jerome Kern.

Wise Publications
London/New York/Sydney

Exclusive Distributors:
Music Sales Limited
8/9 Frith Street, London W1V 5TZ, England.
Music Sales Pty Limited
120 Rothschild Avenue, Rosebery, NSW 2018, Australia.

This book © Copyright 1990 by
Wise Publications
Order No. AM80268
ISBN 0.7119.2337.X

Design and art direction by Mike Bell
Cover illustration by Mark Thomas
Compiled by Peter Evans
Music arranged by Frank Booth
Music processed by Musicprint
Typeset by Capital Setters

Music Sales' complete catalogue lists thousands of
titles and is free from your local music
shop, or direct from Music Sales Limited.
Please send a cheque/postal order for £1.50 for postage to:
Music Sales Limited, 8/9 Frith Street, London W1V 5TZ.

A Fine Romance

Music by Jerome Kern
Words by Dorothy Fields

All The Things You Are

Music by Jerome Kern
Words by Oscar Hammerstein II

Moderately, with expression

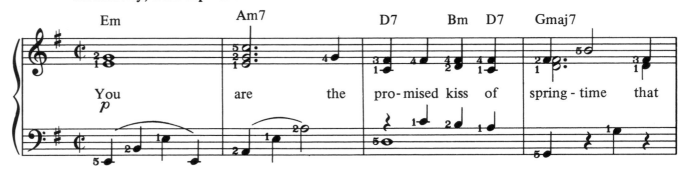

You are the pro-mised kiss of spring-time that

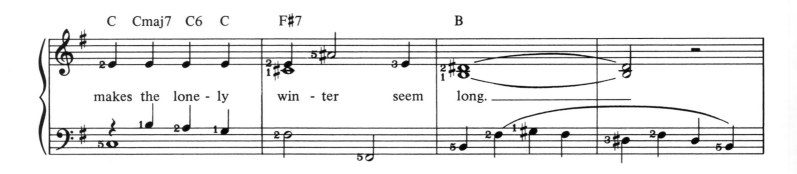

makes the lone-ly win-ter seem long.

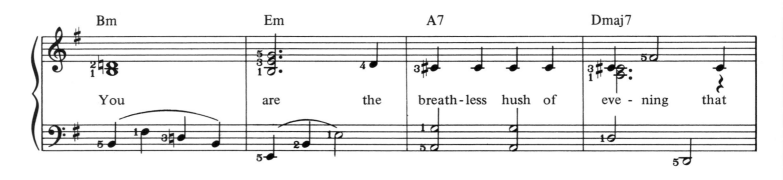

You are the breath-less hush of eve-ning that

trem-bles on the brink of a love-ly song You are the

Can't Help Lovin' Dat Man

Music by Jerome Kern
Words by Oscar Hammerstein II

Dearly Beloved

Music by Jerome Kern
Words by Johnny Mercer

I'm Old Fashioned

Music by Jerome Kern
Words by Johnny Mercer

I've Told Ev'ry Little Star

Music by Jerome Kern
Words by Oscar Hammerstein II

I Won't Dance

Music by Jerome Kern
Words by Oscar Hammerstein II, Dorothy Fields

Pick Yourself Up

Music by Jerome Kern
Words by Dorothy Fields

Long Ago And Far Away

Music by Jerome Kern
Words by Ira Gershwin

Lovely To Look At

Music by Jerome Kern
Words by Dorothy Fields & Jimmy McHugh

The Folks Who Live On The Hill

Music by Jerome Kern
Words by Oscar Hammerstein II

The Last Time I Saw Paris

Music by Jerome Kern
Words by Oscar Hammerstein II

Ol' Man River

Music by Jerome Kern
Words by Oscar Hammerstein II

Git a lit - tle drunk an' you land in jail.

Ah gits wea - ry an' sick of try - in', Ah'm

tired of liv - in' an' skeered of dy - in', But

ol' man ri - ver, he jus' keeps roll - in' a - long.

- long.

Smoke Gets In Your Eyes

Music by Jerome Kern
Words by Otto Harbach

Moderately, with expression

They asked me how I knew my true love was true. _____ I of course re-plied, some-thing here in-side, can-not be de-nied.

The Song Is You

Music by Jerome Kern
Words by Oscar Hammerstein II

They Didn't Believe Me

Music by Jerome Kern
Words by Herbert Reynolds

The Way You Look Tonight

Music by Jerome Kern
Words by Dorothy Fields

Printed and bound in Great Britain by
Caligraving Limited Thetford Norfolk

9/97(28914)